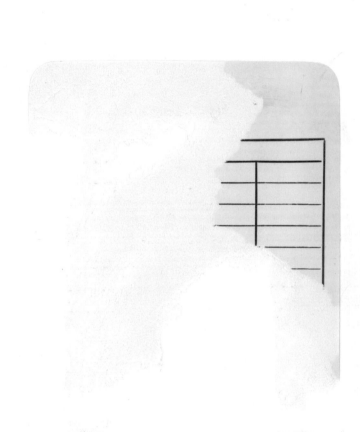

The Catholic Priest

HIS TRAINING AND MINISTRY

The Catholic

Priest
HIS TRAINING AND MINISTRY

A Picture Story
by
JACK ENGEMAN

Foreword by
Richard Cardinal Cushing
Archbishop of Boston

LOTHROP, LEE AND SHEPARD CO., INC.
NEW YORK

Contents

© 1961 by Jack Engeman
Library of Congress Catalog Card Number 61-15445
Printed in the United States of America

Foreword

teresting and appealing way, by affording close-up pictorial glimpses of the daily routine of the seminary and the religious novitiates.

The obvious purpose of the book is to arouse interest in the environment in which young people prepare for the service of the Church. Thus it becomes a welcome addition to efforts being made on so many other fronts to find the vocations which will be needed in ever-increasing numbers if the Church is to bring its divinely-appointed mission into relation with the needs of the age in which we live.

'The Catholic Priest — His Training and Ministry' is comprehensive and true to life. Its appeal is universal, and in correspondence with the needs of the Church as a whole, rather than with the particular vocational program of any one group. By itself it will not be the answer to the problem of finding vocations; but it will certainly open the way into the minds and hearts of thousands of young men who will not be reached otherwise. Many who might open this book out of curiosity will examine it from cover to cover and will derive from it the background against which the interviews of vocation directors will have greater significance.

I am happy to recommend this book as authentic and correctly inspired. I hope to make use of it in my own efforts to find vocations for the diocesan priesthood and for the many religious communities with whom I am associated in the work of saving souls.

Richard Cardinal Cushing

Archbishop of Boston

It is quite in conformity with the trend of modern education to look to photography as a means of stimulating vocations. This is what has been done in this book entitled 'The Catholic Priest — His Training and Ministry.' It introduces us to the life of those who are preparing for the priesthood and religious life in an in-

Dedication

To the men of the Roman Catholic priesthood, men who have dedicated themselves to a profession that is at once in time yet timeless, lofty yet lowly, unique and singular in its purpose yet all-embracing; for their field of labor is wherever they can work for the greater glory of God.

Acknowledgments

First of all, I would like to express my gratitude to two members of the Society of Jesus, the Reverend William M. J. Driscoll and the Reverend Richard A. Kenna, who graciously directed and aided me in this project and who are responsible for the text and captions, which describe the life of the Catholic seminarian and priest.

I would also like to express my gratitude to the Rectors, professors and students of the many seminaries I visited for their kind cooperation and assistance.

Finally, my sincere thanks to my close friends who inspired me to do this work and encouraged me throughout its undertaking.

September 1961   Jack Engeman

Introduction

THE Catholic Church looks upon its priests first of all as men, but men of God, men who have been made instruments of the Divine Will. God's mission is entrusted to a human person; Christ's sacrifice is now offered by a human minister; divine forgiveness of sins is exercised by a human individual; human hands dispense divine sacraments; the Word of God is preached through the mouth of a man. It is through the office of the priesthood that these divine priestly powers are bestowed upon a human person. Not conferred even upon the angels, such privileges and powers are given to men.

The priest remains a man, though raised to the dignity of this divine calling. A mediator between God and men, called by God, he intercedes for men before God. And since the priest remains a man, he knows the weakness of fallen human nature, and he can sympathize with his fellow men. Since he remains a man, the priest must gain all his strength, confidence and his very Priesthood from Jesus Christ, the God-man, the Eternal High Priest.

It is the purpose of the following pages to depict the training which the priest receives in the seminaries for this divine calling, and graphically to present him in his ministries when, standing between God and men, he brings God to men, and men to God, and gives himself to both.

Part One

The Secular or Diocesan Clergy

THE Secular or Diocesan Clergy are those priests who undertake their ministries living independently in the world, either alone, or in small groups in the parish rectory. Their work is mainly parochial. They are not bound by rule as the "regular" or "religious" clergy are. The secular clergy are the normal clergy of the Catholic Church, and are bound by no vows except, by implication, that of celibacy. The secular priest promises canonical obedience to his Bishop and may own and enjoy his own property.

Preparatory Seminary and College for Diocesan Priests

PREPARATORY seminaries for youth training to be diocesan priests are schools of general education for boys from 12 to 18, embarking upon their vocation for the diocesan priesthood. Technically, one of these preparatory seminaries should be conducted as part of every diocesan seminary, but not necessarily on the same premises. Sometimes a larger preparatory seminary services several dioceses.

The young man who desires to become a diocesan priest may enter after graduation from grammar school, and pursue his high-school training in the preparatory seminary. He then stays two more years at the same seminary, or moves to another, where he takes his first two years of college education.

Although he receives normal high school education in the preparatory seminary and college, he also receives spiritual education, and is taught how to pray, to grow in the spiritual life and union with God, and to start the development of his priestly ideas and ideals.

Upon arrival at the seminary the young student is greeted and briefed by the Prefect of Studies.

High school classes are the usual order of the day except for Sundays and the weekly holiday.

During out-of-door periods, the seminarians may choose or be assigned, to work around the grounds—

—or, if not otherwise assigned may choose to engage in a variety of sports.

During recreation after the evening meal, many seminarians walk about the grounds in quiet conversation.

A familiar scene in any school: rain, sunshine or snow, the students head for class!

All the needs of the seminarians, even their bi-weekly hair cuts, are provided on the seminary grounds.

Likewise, at appropriate times, almost every type of recreation is available to relax their young minds.

And, as the day in the seminary begins with prayer, so it ends with prayer before the Blessed Sacrament.

The Major Seminary

Philosophy

AFTER finishing his first two years of college in the preparatory seminary, the seminarian studying for the diocesan priesthood moves to the major seminary.

The first two years of his studies in the major seminary consist of intensified courses in scholastic philosophy and the necessary courses for his college degree.

The seminarian studies and digests the great thoughts of the past. Aristotle, Plato, St. Augustine, Thomas Aquinas, Descartes, Kant, and Marx—the complete Western intellectual tradition is the field of his attention during his two years of the study of philosophy.

He likewise is instructed in Sacred Liturgy, Sacred Chant and the Scriptures. His spiritual training is continued, and his union with God is made more intense. It is a two-year period of intellectual and personal maturing.

The Major Seminary is a home where the young seminarian enjoys the warm association of older priests.

Each seminarian has his own private room where he spends many hours in study and prayer.

The library provides ample literature on all subjects related to his coming ministry.

A class of major seminarians takes its final examination in Natural Theology, the proof of God's existence by reason.

From meditation the seminarians learn to grow in their knowledge and love of Christ.

Although studies are important, prayer, or union with God, always takes first place.

Other college subjects leading to his Bachelor's Degree supplement the seminarian's study of philosophy.

A frequent scene between classes in good weather.

During May especially, the seminarians gather to pray and honor the Blessed Virgin Mary.

The development of the whole man, in body as well as mind, demands vigorous exercise.

During recreation some prefer just to sit and talk— —while others like to play cards.

On rainy days, the shuffleboard provides easy relaxation.

The memory of saintly priests who have gone to their reward provides inspiration.

During most meals, a seminarian is assigned to read at table—

—but on holidays and special occasions, permission is given to talk.

Constant union with God is the source of a seminarian's strength.

The Major Seminary
Sacred Theology

FOUR years of Sacred Theology complete the major seminary course for those studying for the diocesan priesthood. The course of training includes Dogmatic, Moral and Pastoral Theology, Apologetics, Ecclesiastical History, Canon Law and Sacred Chant. Intensified studies of the Scriptures and great stress on the art of Sacred Eloquence are likewise included in the program.

Since the priest is ordained to offer sacrifice, to baptize, to join in marriage, he studies the Sacred Liturgy. Apart from actual courses, preparation and practice for this liturgical side of his priestly life engages considerable time in his seminary career. And, he also learns by experience to join in the corporate worship of the Church.

During these four years of Sacred Theology, the young diocesan seminarian receives minor and major orders, and at the end of his fourth year is ordained to the Sacred Priesthood of Christ.

Father Rector welcomes three new arrivals for the study of Sacred Theology.

First day of class reunites old friends and brings new acquaintances.

Although the old grind of class starts once again, the seminarian's goal, the priesthood, is in sight.

Accurate note-taking is essential to recall the substance of each lecture.

Every seminarian must practice in order that he become a good public speaker.

A class in the rites of Holy Sacrifice of the Mass.

The periodical room,

the rare books and special collection stacks,

and the general reading room of the library
provide ample study material.

Changing social conditions require seminarians to possess a speaking knowledge of modern languages.

Scripture students examine a scale model of Herod's Temple.

Grace is said in common before meals.

Seminarians are assigned in regular rotation to serve their brother seminarians at meals.

An enjoyable conversation follows the Rector's signal that talking is allowed at dinner.

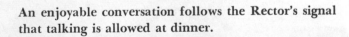

No preacher will ever have more difficult circumstances or a more critical audience than the seminarian preaching at dinner.

In the prayer-hall seminarians gather for prayer, meditation and spiritual reading.

A seminarian reads a spiritual book under the supervision of a faculty member in the prayer-hall.

Theological faculty members teach by their prayerful example as well as by their lectures.

An ever-growing and maturing love of the Blessed Virgin Mary is nourished by daily devotions.

Each evening finds the seminarians gathered in the chapel to thank God for the graces of that day.

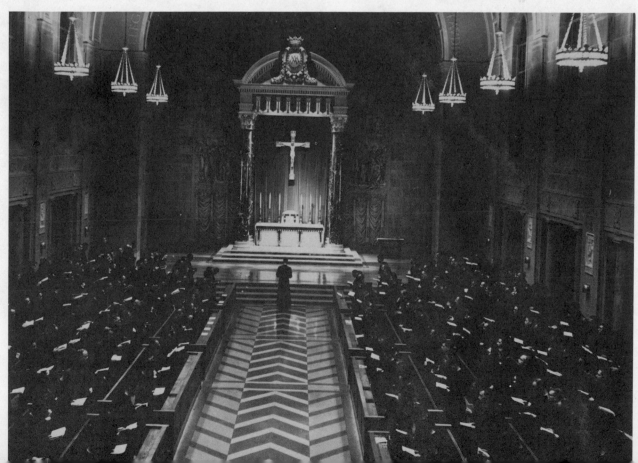

Silence is observed by the seminarians on the way from the dining room to the chapel for a short visit after meals.

Informal conversations are not infrequent between the Rector and the seminarians.

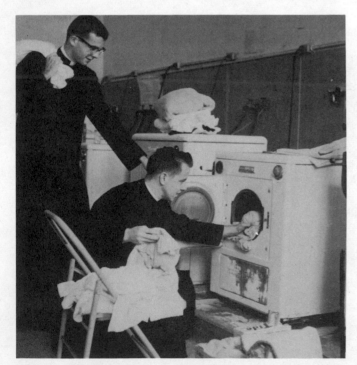

"Do-it-yourself" laundry is a great convenience to the seminarians.

Even the hobbies of the seminarian can be of use in his future ministry.

Some seminarians like outdoor manual work.

Other seminarians enjoy perfecting talents they brought with them to the seminary . . .

. . . or enjoy an informal get-together for some old-fashioned harmony.

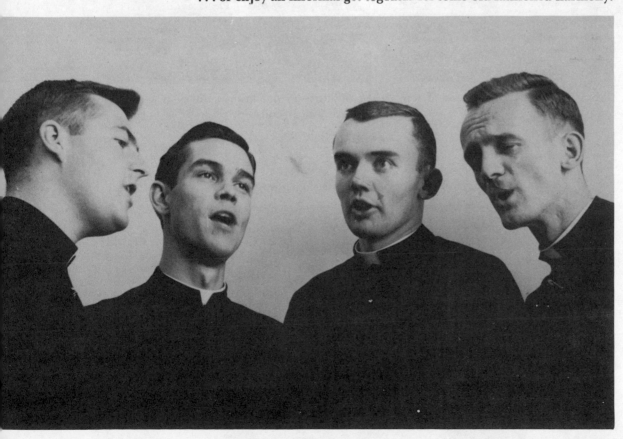

One of the professors takes time to relax.

"Breaks" between classes afford a few moments of leisure during a busy morning.

In small, informal groups, there is a great exchange of ideas and friendship.

Apostolic works on a holiday: visiting hospitals,

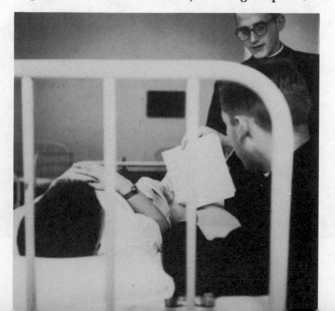

nearby orphan homes,

convalescent homes,

or teaching catechism.

Choir members spend many hours in rehearsal.

Others enjoy a band session.

Some seminarians find the game of chess very relaxing.

Some seminarians like to help in the physical maintenance of the seminary.

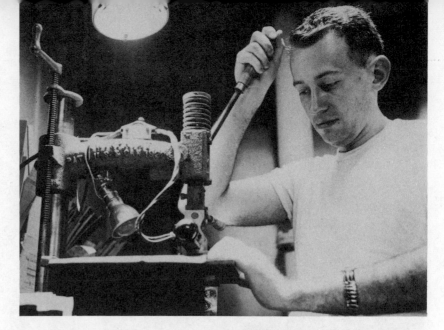

Still others have frequent practice sessions in the sign language for the deaf.

In the seminary "Mission Store" statues, books and other religious articles are sold.

Changes in the daily order and various new assignments are published on the seminary bulletin board.

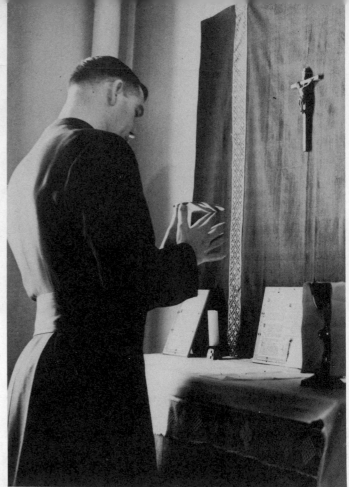

A Deacon privately practices saying Mass in a small chapel.

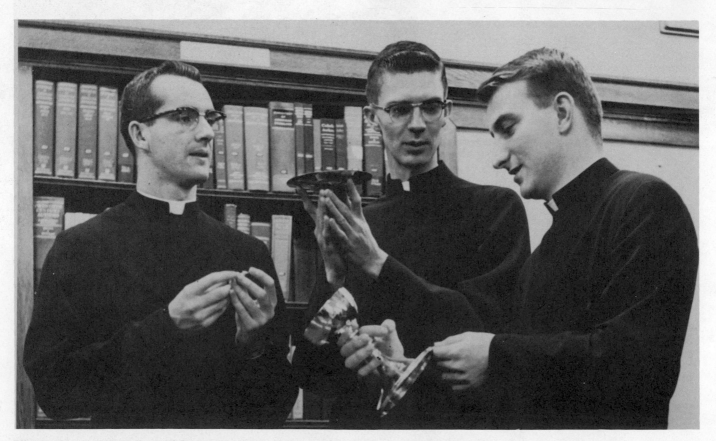

Three theologians who will be ordained shortly practice the rites of the Holy Sacrifice of the Mass.

A dream nears fulfillment as the seminarian selects
his own personal chalice,

is measured for his ordination cassock,

and reads the breviary for the last several weeks as
a Deacon.

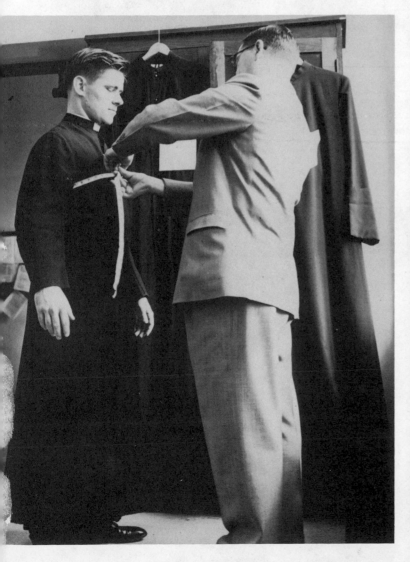

During the seminarian's course in the major seminary, he frequently partici-
pates in ecclesiastical functions at the local cathedral.

Usually several seminarians from each diocese are sent each year to study in Rome at the North American College . . .

. . . where, overlooking the Eternal City and the great Cathedral of St. Peter's, their priestly zeal is enkindled.

Older candidates for the priesthood also have a seminary in Rome exclusively for their own training.

A portion of the great lecture hall at the Gregorian University, Rome, where seminarians gather from all over the world to study Sacred Theology.

Ordination

Minor and Major Orders

ACTUAL Ordination to the priesthood is the last of seven steps, the seven Orders which the Church confers on her priests.

The rite of tonsure, which prepares for the reception of minor and major orders, is performed by the Bishop cutting the hair of the candidate's head in front, behind, on both sides and on the crown.

The four Minor Orders, received after clerical tonsure, are Porter, Lector, Exorcist and Acolyte.

Tonsure.

The call for Minor Orders.

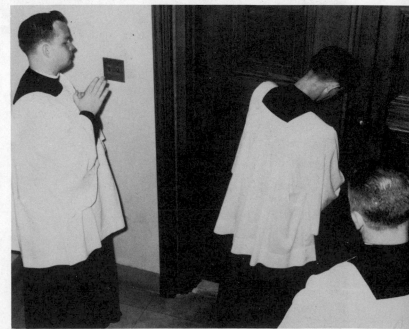

Exercising the Order of Porter.

37

The Subdeaconate

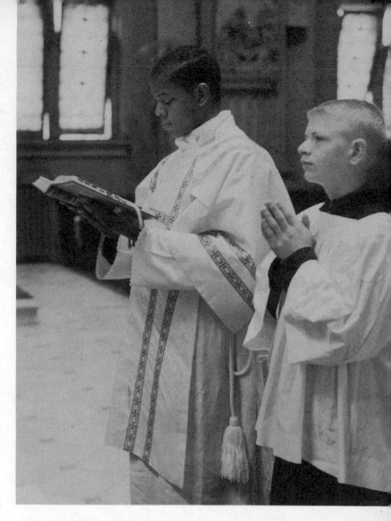

THE Subdeaconate is the lowest of the Major Orders. It is of ecclesiastical institution, and it is an Order which involves, in the Western Church, the obligation of perpetual celibacy. The Divine Office must likewise be recited by the subdeacon.

The subdeacon is allowed to sing the Epistle at Solemn High Mass, and bring the vessels to the altar. He is also permitted the function of holding the paten during the canon, and gives the kiss of peace to the choir.

The Subdeacon chants the Epistle at Solemn High Mass.

Subdeacons await the call of the Bishop to be ordained to the Deaconate.

The Deaconate

THE Major Order of Deacon is bestowed by the laying-on of the Bishop's hands as he says the following appropriate words: "Receive the Holy Spirit . . ." The Bishop also hands over to the candidate the stole, the dalmatic and the gospel book. The Deacon can administer Holy Communion and baptize solemnly with permission, should it be necessary. He also can assist the Celebrant at Solemn High Mass. The order of Deacon is the second of the major orders.

The Deacon assists the Celebrant at Solemn High Mass.

The Priest Is Ordained

CHRIST it is who ordains priests. He it is Who has invited young men to consecrate their lives to God and to the salvation of souls. The Bishop, acting for Christ and as His instrument, places his hands on the head of each Deacon and invokes the Holy Spirit. But, Christ it is Who ordains, Christ it is Who sends the Holy Spirit, Christ it is Who officially welcomes them into that long line of priests extending back two thousand years to the Last Supper, and that shall be projected into the future "until He comes."

And after Ordination, what a change! To the eyes of men, Christ has made them leaders in His Church to carry on the work of His Redemption; in their souls, Christ has radically transformed them by a spiritual mark, the mark of the priesthood of Christ, which like His own wounds, is indestructible for all eternity.

And the priest's powers—power over the very Body of Christ, power over the Mystical Body of Christ—are all designed to attend to the spiritual need of souls from birth to death, and lead them to Eternal Life.

What unspeakable joy fills the soul and the heart of a new priest! And, although he knows as a man he himself is weak and unequal to the task, nevertheless his anxiety is swallowed up in perfect confidence in Christ Who said to him personally: "You have not chosen Me, but I have chosen you. . . ."

During the sung Litanies, the Deacons who are about to be ordained priests prostrate themselves before the altar.

After the Bishop has laid both hands on the head of every Ordinand in turn, the same is done by all the priests present.

Each newly ordained priest washes off the oil which the Bishop used to consecrate his hands.

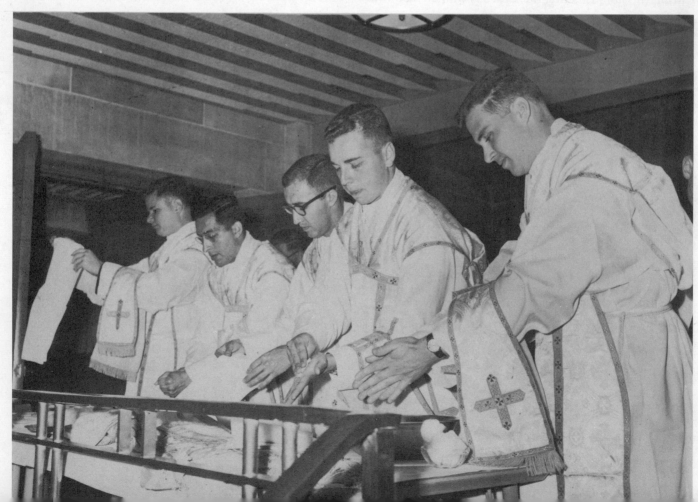

42

Together with the ordaining Bishop each new priest con-celebrates, and offers with the Bishop his first Mass.

After receiving Communion from the hands of the Bishop, each new priest takes a sip of wine.

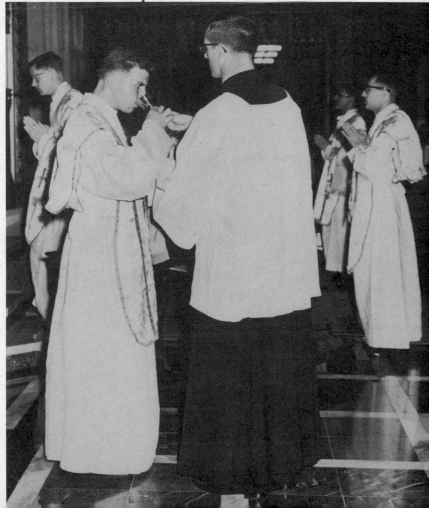

Mass over, the new priest gives his first blessing to his relatives and friends.

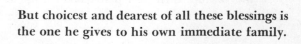

But choicest and dearest of all these blessings is
the one he gives to his own immediate family.

First Mass

AFTER the new priest's ordination he returns home, and surrounded by a host of relatives and friends, he takes Bread and Wine in his own hands, and for the first time in solemn fashion, consecrates them into the Body and Blood of Christ, and offers Christ in His own Sacrifice to God the Father.

What a joy and blessing!

The Gloria of a first Solemn High Mass.

The newly-ordained priest, as celebrant of the Solemn High Mass, is incensed after the Offertory.

The new priest holds aloft the consecrated host for the adoration of the faithful.

After his first Solemn High Mass, the new priest, the other officers of the mass, the preacher, the local pastor, and those present in the sanctuary, pose on the front steps of the local parish church.

The Ministry of Secular Priests

THE ministry of Secular Priests is concerned mainly with the cell unit of the Church, the parish. Living with two or three other priests in the parish rectory, or by himself, should the parish be a small one, he performs the ordinary functions of the priesthood: offering the Holy Sacrifice of the Mass for the people, bringing the sacraments of Christ to them, teaching them the Word of God, and being their father and guide.

Some priests in almost every diocese are engaged, however, in activities other than direct parish work, labors which are necessary for the organization of the diocese or for social or other works therein.

The following pages are a brief sketch of the work of the diocesan priest in the parish, and show you some of the other activities in which he may engage.

Sunday sermons and mid-week devotional sermons are regular functions of the parish priest.

The parish priest vests and ascends to the altar daily to pray for his people.

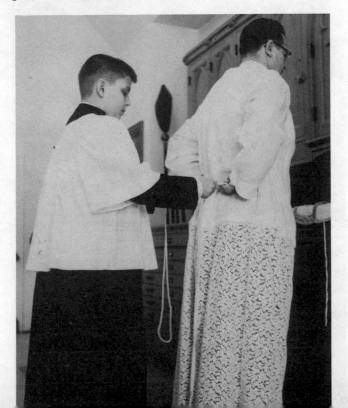

Infant baptisms are usually performed on Sunday afternoon.

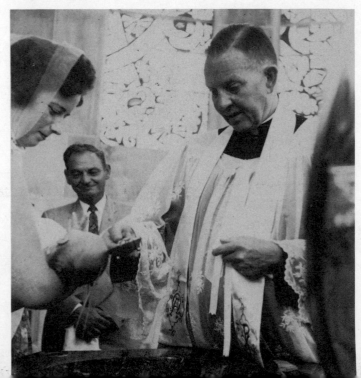

Saturday afternoons and evenings are the usual times for the administration of the Sacrament of Penance.

One of the greatest joys of the priesthood is the distribution of Holy Communion.

The Bishop is the ordinary minister of the Sacrament of Confirmation. However, the local pastor may confirm his own subjects in case there is danger of death.

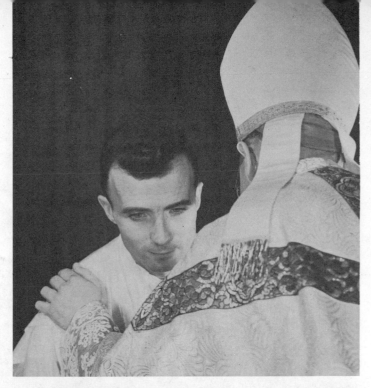

The Bishop alone can administer the Sacrament of Holy Orders, because he alone possesses the fullness of the priesthood.

In danger of death the priest is called to administer the Sacrament of Extreme Unction.

The priest is the official witness of the Church at marriages and blesses them.

A Day in the Life of a Secular Priest

The curate checks over the details of the coming day with the pastor after breakfast.

Frequent visits to classrooms of the parish school are part of the parish priest's function.

The parish priest can frequently pass on valuable tips for sports to his young flock.

After the children have made their first confession, Father watches them practice for the reception of their First Holy Communion.

The devotion and trust which the parish priest enjoys among his flock is caught in the expression of these two young school children.

The officers of the Parent-Teacher Association discuss their next meeting with Father.

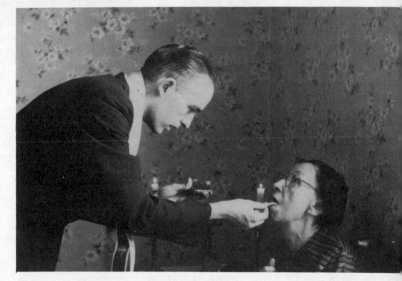

Sick calls are frequent in the daily life of a parish priest.

Private instructions in the faith are given to those who are contemplating becoming Catholics.

51

The president and officers of a local CYO go over their program with the parish priest, their moderator.

The Superintendent of the Diocesan Parochial Schools makes one of his periodic visitations.

Reception of new members into the parish Sodality of Our Lady.

Chatting with devoted parishioners.

Diocesan priests appear frequently on television and radio programs concerning the Faith.

Almost every diocese has a diocesan newspaper, under the direction of a diocesan priest.

The Diocesan Director of the CYO sponsors frequent city-wide activities for youth.

The Holy Name Society, under the leadership of the parish priest, is a vigorous spiritual force in the parish.

Some dioceses conduct missions in foreign lands, to which they send secular priests.

Some diocesan priests are elevated to the bishopric. They may be given special assignments, such as being made rector of a large seminary.

Most Bishops and Archbishops, however, are assigned to a particular diocese to govern, or are appointed as assisting Bishops in a particular diocese.

In his daily recitation of the **Divine Office**, the official prayer of the Church, as well as **in his** private prayers and sacrifices, the diocesan priest prays for his people, thus fulfilling his privilege and obligation.

Part Two

The Religious Clergy

THE Religious Clergy, or the Regulars, are those clerics who take the three vows of Religion: Poverty, Chastity and Obedience. They live in a community, according to a way of life, or a rule. In this they differ from the Secular or the Diocesan Clergy.

A "Religious Order," in ordinary speech, is any ecclesiastical society which the Church calls a "Religious Institute." A "Religious Institute" is a society of men (or women) which has been

approved by ecclesiastical superiors. In it, the members, in conformity with the special laws of their groups, take the vows of religion, and in this way tend to evangelical perfection. Every religious institute must receive definite and formal approval from either the Holy See or a Bishop.

A list of the clerical Religious Institutes in the United States may be found at the end of this book.

Religious Preparatory Seminary

As IN the case with the diocesan clergy, many religious institutes conduct a preparatory seminary, covering the ground of a boy's high-school career.

While the intellectual stress is placed on high-school academic subjects and particularly on Latin, close spiritual direction is given to the prospective candidate and the spirit of the religious institute to which he aspires becomes part of his everyday thinking.

It is not infrequent that the first seeds of a priestly vocation are implanted in conversation between a young boy and the Sister who teaches him in grammar school.

By kindly interest and direction, the young boy's local Pastor helps him make his decision regarding his vocation.

The new aspirant is given a warm welcome at the Preparatory Seminary.

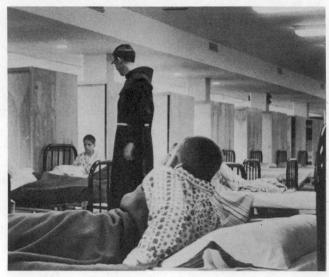

The young seminarian's day starts early, but its rewards are great.

The greatest and the choicest of these rewards is the daily reception of Our Lord in Holy Communion.

High school studies are just as puzzling to a seminarian as to anyone else.

And the minor seminarian, like every other high school boy, loves sports.

While the body of the young man is being fed, spiritual reading provides nourishment for his soul.

Individual spiritual guidance is frequent and always close at hand in a religious minor seminary.

Religious Novitiate and College Studies

Every religious institute must have a novitiate, or a period of spiritual formation, after which the novice professes his first vows, either temporary or perpetual. The length of the novitiate varies according to the constitution of the individual religious institute, but it must be of at least one year's duration. Separate apartments are provided for the novices, and they are cut off entirely from the professed religious of the institute. The daily order of novices in all religious institutes is about the same. He rises early in the morning, visits the Blessed Sacrament, makes a meditation, and then assists at Mass and receives Holy Communion. After breakfast, the novice follows a daily order which is broken up into a number of small duties planned to advance him in the spirit of unselfishness.

The hidden life of Jesus for so many years at Nazareth is the model for the novice. He learns the meaning of daily spiritual practices: meditations, examination of conscience, litanies, rosaries, spiritual reading, and so forth. He spends a good deal of time in humble labor, indoors and outdoors. His friend and spiritual father is the Master of Novices, and his fellow novices are his brothers.

Sooner than possible the noviceship has sped by, and it has readied him to bind himself to Christ forever. When that wonderful Vow Day arrives, he pronounces his vows of poverty, chastity and obedience. Thus ends the first stage of his new life for Christ.

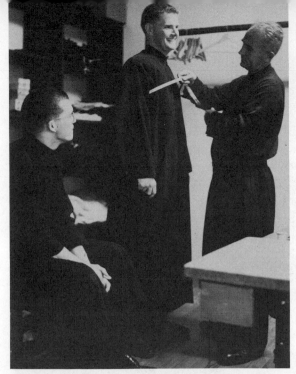

One of the first big thrills of the noviceship is when the young novice is measured for his first religious habit.

The novice strives to dedicate his life completely to Christ, but also acquires great devotion to the Blessed Virgin Mary.

Much time is spent every day in the chapel by the novices, starting with early morning Mass and Communion.

The very heart of any religious institute is always conveyed to the novices by the Master of Novices.

The reading of the lives of saints and ascetical works strengthens the young novice's zeal and stimulates imitation.

Daily meditation and examination of conscience are among the spiritual activities of the novice.

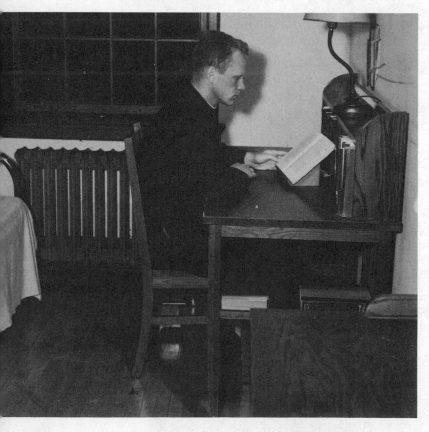

The rosary is recited by the novices daily.

Two novices making the Stations of the Cross on the novitiate grounds.

Some religious institutes require the novices to recite the Divine Office daily.

Novices perform humble tasks daily: mopping the corridor floors,

setting up the tables in the refectory;

washing the dishes after meals.

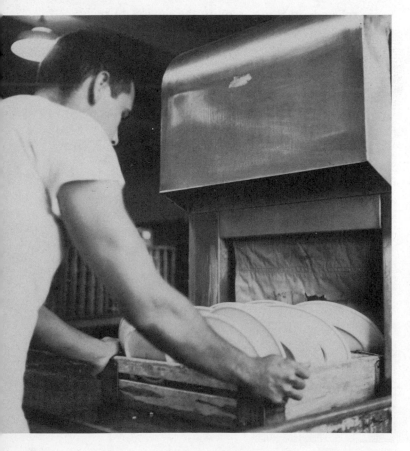

Some novices visit non-Catholic families in nearby parishes to spread the Faith.

Novices always welcome seasonal athletics: swimming in the summer,

football in the fall,

hockey in the winter.

In any religious family, the young religious acquires piety and zeal through occasional conversation with the professed fathers.

Family visiting days are welcome and happy days in the noviceship, and the memory of them is made permanent by the camera.

A novice reads, and his fellow novices serve their brother novices at table.

Novices at the end of evening recreation gather at the door about to return to their evening duties.

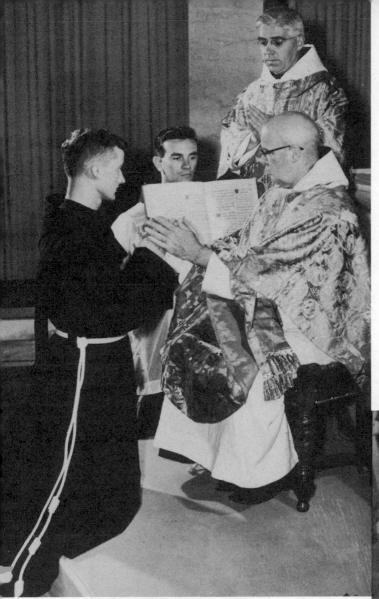

At the end of his noviceship, the young religious pronounces his first public vows of poverty, chastity and obedience.

In his vows, the religious gives himself entirely to Christ; and in Holy Communion, he receives back Christ's own gift to him, Himself.

After his vows, among the first to congratulate him are his own brothers in religion.

Some religious institutes present a copy of their rule book and a crucifix to the newly professed on their vow day.

A proud father captures the happiness of Vow Day in a family picture.

The vows of the new religious gives joy to his human family;

and they give joy, too, to his religious family.

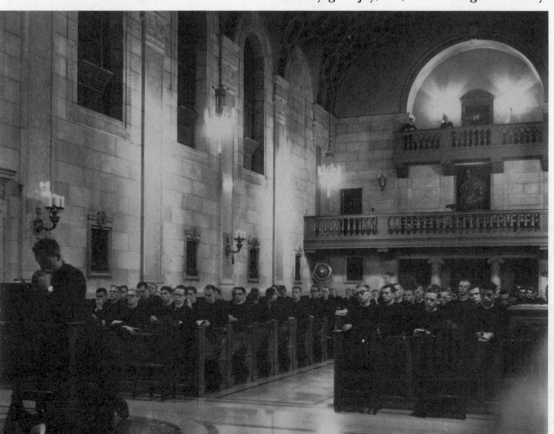

Religious College Studies

ALL clerical religious institutes provide collegiate studies for those who aspire to be priests, the first two years of which are very similar to the first two years of the collegiate studies for the secular clergy.

It depends upon the individual religious institute whether the noviceship precedes or comes after all or some of these collegiate studies.

The weekly Latin theme is of great assistance to the young seminarian in mastering this necessary language.

Small classes and personal attention stimulate individual initiative.

The seminarian must know how to use books effectively; he learns this in these early days.

Teaching catechism, visiting hospitals and prisons, provide religious seminarians with apostolic opportunities a-plenty.

Students learn by listening and reading; they also learn by discussing and analyzing.

In the midst of all these studies, however, there is always time for meditation, prayer, the stations and the beads.

Analyzing current events in relation to his studies gives the student a critical judgment.

From the end of evening recreation to night prayers is a good time for private study.

The young religious seminarian is frequently assigned to serve one of the fathers at Holy Mass. Here a seminarian checks the Mass assignment board.

The young members of religious communities are trained to sing for liturgical functions.

Visiting days are happy days for the seminarian and his visitors, young and old.

During outdoor periods religious seminarians may choose to get their exercise by playing sports, or find opportunities for physical work.

Religious Major Seminary

Philosophy

FOR the next two or three years, the young religious seminarian studies philosophy. The whole universe comes under the scrutiny of his natural reason and he seeks to answer the eternal question "why?". He studies the great thinkers of history, and learns how their minds struggled with that question. Soon Plato, Aristotle, St. Augustine, St. Thomas, Suarez, Kant, and their successors, commentators and adversaries become familiar to him.

Philosophy is a preparation for the young religious seminarian's later theological studies. Simply put, it teaches him to think, and not merely to absorb thoughts.

This is a period of hard, scholarly labor spent in an atmosphere of peace and friendship. But the life of study in the seminary during these years does not exclude time for fervent prayer and spiritual growth. Truly these years in this portion of his seminary training bring a steady advance in spiritual maturity and intellectual competence.

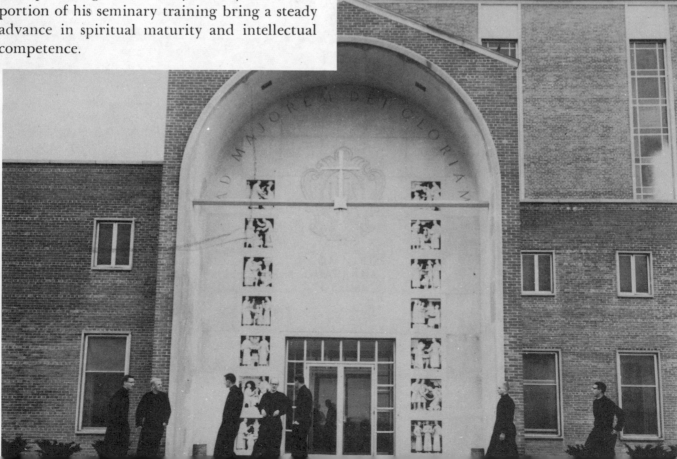

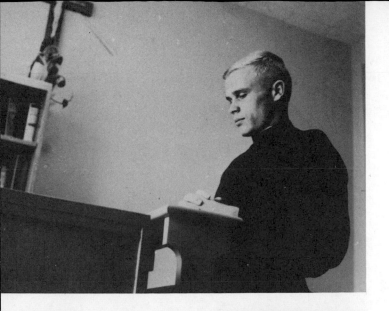

Meditation each morning strengthens the young religious in his love of Christ and his desire to imitate Him.

In the quiet of his own room, a "philosopher" is able to ponder and absorb the great thoughts of the past.

Quizzical looks imply a thinking mind, and the purpose of philosophy is to teach these seminarians to think properly.

With a major in philosophy, the seminarian also has electives in mathematics, languages, history and social studies.

Modern technique helps the seminarian to perfect the necessary art of Sacred Eloquence.

An adequate knowledge of the physical sciences is a necessity of the Space Age and for the priest who will deal with educated men from every professional background.

Discussion groups between the seminarians and the faculty fathers treat of special problems not included in the courses.

The fathers who teach philosophy on the faculty are available for private consultation and discussion.

"Bless us, O Lord, and these Thy gifts, which we are about to receive from Thy bounty, through Christ Our Lord. Amen."

The thoughts of God and the thoughts of men slowly penetrate the soul of the religious seminarian in silent meditation.

Rooms are dusted and beds are made each morning after breakfast.

For local news, changes in assignment, order of the day, the seminarian consults the bulletin board.

Some of the seminarians teach public-school children catechism on released time.

And outside of class both the seminarians and their pupils have a lot of real good fun.

Another way of praising God is to teach children to sing hymns, as this seminarian is doing.

With each happy visit parents and their sons in religion find themselves closer than ever before.

The talents found among religious seminarians are many and varied. Some seminaries can boast of a jazz band.

The seminary quartet makes itself available for all occasions requiring musical entertainment.

On holidays, the young religious are frequently allowed to enjoy picnics, outdoors or indoors.

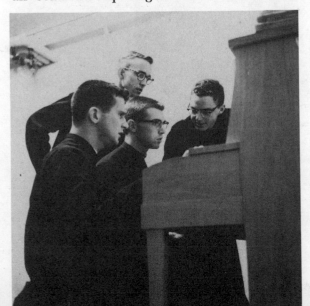

A religious philosopher may be assigned to help in the preparation of meals.

In addition to sports and work for physical exercise, many philosophers like to walk and talk.

At the end of his course of philosophy, the religious seminarian finds that he has grown "in wisdom, age, and grace," before God and man.

Religious
Major Seminary

Theology

FOUR of the best years of the religious seminarian's life are now devoted to theology, the science of God.

Up to now, he has studied the world as man's reasoning power can understand it. Now as a theologian he begins to study God and the world as God has revealed Himself and the world to man.

Dogmatic Theology, Moral Theology, Canon Law, Scripture, Apologetics, Church History, Rites—all of these courses are included in his four years of study. And in his spare time he carefully acts out the ceremonies of the Mass which soon will be real.

His studies in theology begin and what a magnificent vista they unfold for him; what a sense of expectancy they bring as the religious theologian begins his final step towards the altar!

Rev. Father Rector and some of the faculty welcome an incoming first-year theologian to the seminary.

How does one study theology? By reading and analyzing the Sacred Scriptures, the councils of the Church, the early Christian writers, and the great theologians. Hundreds of periodicals and books published each year on theology find their way into the seminary library.

Forceful and committed professors lecture on the great religious truths of the Christian tradition.

Private study in the seminarian's own room is needed to assimilate 2,000 years of Christian tradition. The theologian begins to realize now more than ever that everything he does, including his studies, he does for souls.

Many religious theologians learn several additional languages during their theological studies for use either at home or on the missions in the future; and modern linguistic teaching methods enable them to teach themselves.

The religious theologian enjoys reading the daily newspaper.

At certain times of the year, especially at Christmas time, when both incoming and outgoing mail is heavy at the seminary, seminarians help in sorting out the mail.

Some seminaries of theology conduct correspondence courses in the Catholic faith.

The seminary can frequently be of great service to a small rural community, as, for example, in providing volunteer fire-fighters.

After the theologian returns from outdoor physical work, not only his body, but his mind is relaxed.

A strum and a hum also are relaxing to many.

Week-end preaching by a religious theologian in a public city square attracts an interested crowd of youngsters.

Friendship and understanding win the interest of these children and then they will listen to the word of God.

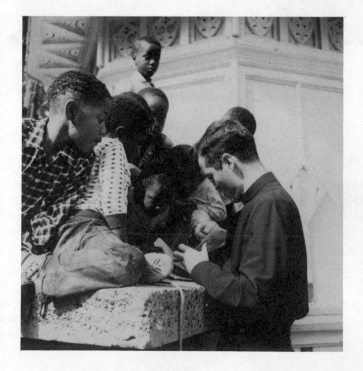

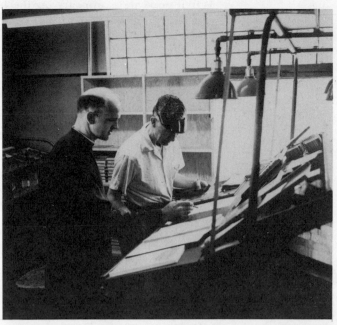

Scientific radio knowledge can be of help in any seminary, and greatly helpful to one going on the missions.

The printed word is a great vehicle for the Gospel. Some seminaries have their own press for publishing articles by the faculty and the seminarians.

Rev. Father Rector confers daily with his appointed representative from the theologians about administrative details.

Choirs in theological seminaries, although sometimes small in number, are well trained.

When good news appears on the bulletin board, you can read it on the face of any theologian.

As ordination approaches for the religious seminarian, he comes to his final classes and examinations in theology.

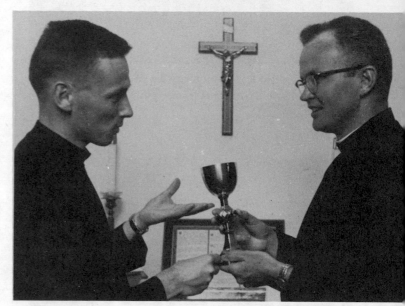

A newly ordained priest instructs a seminarian who will be ordained the next year in the rites of Holy Mass.

Prayer is the heart of the religious life. The religious theologian during his seminary studies spends several hours each day praying privately or in a group. And, at least once a year, separates himself from ordinary concerns to make a retreat. This means that for a period of about a week he devotes himself exclusively to quiet and prayer, dropping all other duties, activities and associations.

Ordination

Minor and Major Orders

LIKE the diocesan priest, the religious priest also receives tonsure, the four minor orders, and the two major orders of Subdeaconate and Deaconate. Depending upon the constitutions of the individual religious institute, all of these take place at their appointed time, and precede ordination to the priesthood.

Finally, the most moving and solemn moment of priestly ordination comes. Through the hands of the Bishop the sacrament of Orders is conferred, making the religious a priest forever.

Tonsure. This is the rite, performed by the Bishop, which prepares the seminarian for minor and major orders.

After the reception of sub-deaconate, the cleric reads the Holy Office daily.

The Deacon may expose the Blessed Sacrament at Solemn Benediction.

Ordination to

At the beginning of the ceremony the Bishop instructs those to be ordained.

The ordaining Bishop prays thus over the prostrate Ordinands: "We beseech Thee, O Lord, hear us: that it may please Thee to bless these chosen ones, to hallow these chosen ones, and to consecrate these chosen ones."

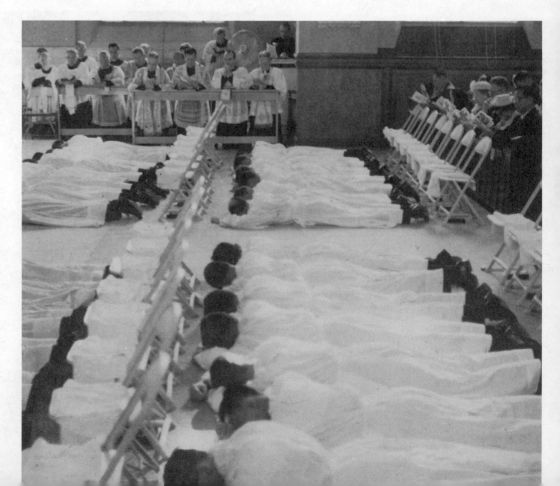

the Priesthood

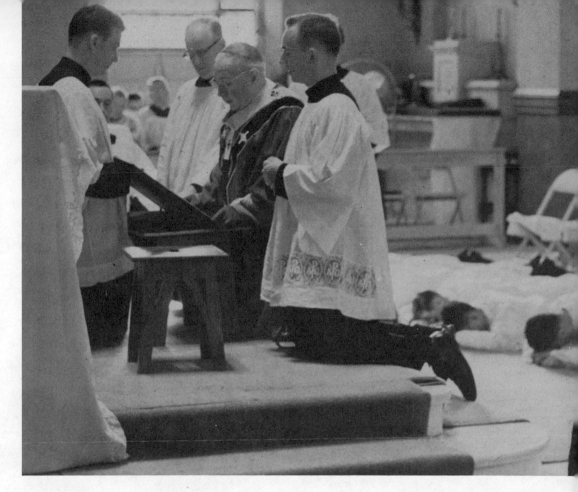

The Bishop then kneels down again while the choir finishes the litany.

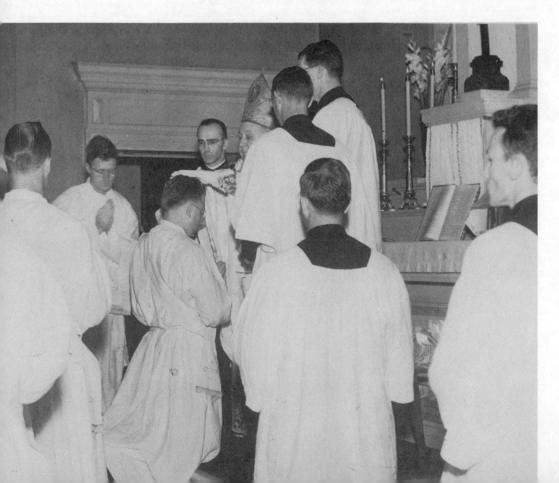

After the Litany of the Saints, all stand, and the Ordinands kneel successively before the Bishop. In silence, the Bishop lays both hands on the head of each Ordinand in turn. The same is done after him by all the priests present.

The Bishop and the Priests keep their right hands extended over the Ordinands while the Bishop prays thus: "Grant, we beseech Thee, Almighty Father, to these Thy servants the dignity of the Priesthood; re-new within them the spirit of holiness, that they may keep the rank in Thy service, which they have received from Thee; and by their conduct may afford a pattern of holy living."

The Bishop, sitting down, vests each new priest with the chasuble, saying: "Take thou the priestly vestment whereby charity is signified; for God is well able to give thee an increase of charity and its perfect works."

The anointing of the new priests' hands by the Bishop.

The newly ordained priests concelebrate with the Bishop.

The first blessing of the newly-ordained religious priests for parents.

During the rest of the day friends and relatives crowd about the newly-ordained priest to receive his blessing and kiss his hands.

The first Solemn High Mass of the newly ordained religious priest in his home parish.

After his first Solemn High Mass, the priest holds a reception and he gives his blessing to parents and friends.

The Ministry
of
Religious Priests

WHEN his seminary years are over and the entire prescribed course completed, the young, newly ordained religious priest may be appointed, according to the constitutions of his religious institute, to any one of a wide variety of posts: working in a parish, preaching retreats and missions, teaching in high schools, colleges and universities, writing and doing research, editing and publishing journals of various types, laboring on the missions—all these and more may be possibilities.

As a parish priest he witnesses marriages . . .

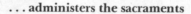

. . . administers the sacraments

. . . and is always at hand to render spiritual service to his parishioners.

Other duties of the parish priests: social work,

work among the underprivileged,

preaching the word of God.

training the parish altar boys,

A noble work of some religious and secular priests is conducting or teaching in seminaries.

Religious priests may give retreats to laymen,

or to school children,

or conduct retreat houses especially for boys.

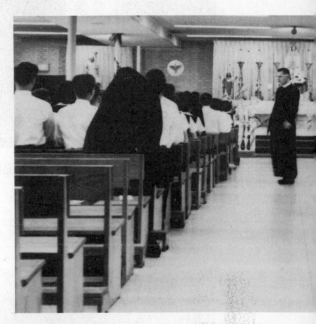

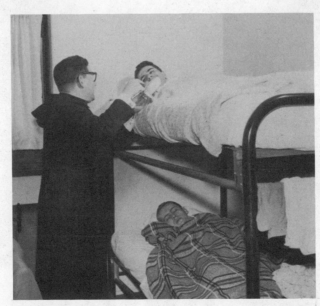

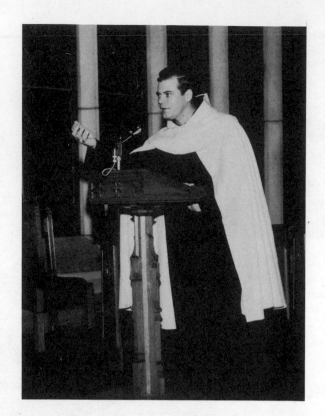

Parish missions are preached by religious priests,

and many give the annual retreats to Religious Women, and also to priests.

Religious priests are assigned to conduct social institutes and labor schools in large industrial areas.

Active priestly work among immigrants gives them the spirit of democracy and saves them from communism.

Some religious institutes work among the colored, either in city parishes or in rural areas.

Information about the Catholic faith may be acquired personally at information centers, or through publications from the Catholic Press. Many religious priests work in both fields.

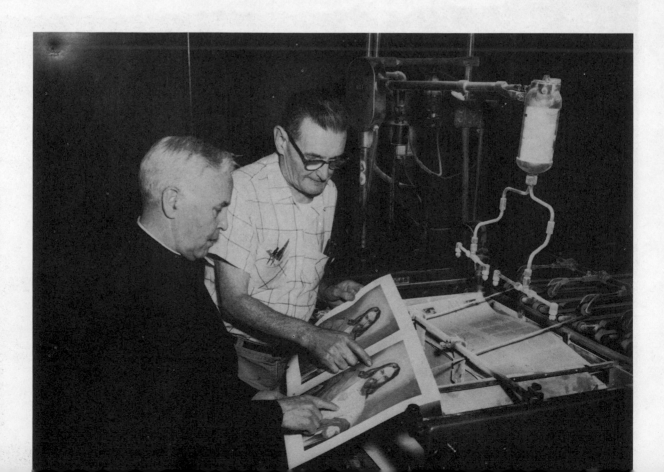

Some priests are assigned to raise funds for the Missions, or for the support of the seminaries of their religious institute, or for the colleges they maintain.

Other assignments:
 . . . writing and research . . .

 . . .leading adult theological discussion groups . . .

 . . . and teaching religion in private schools.

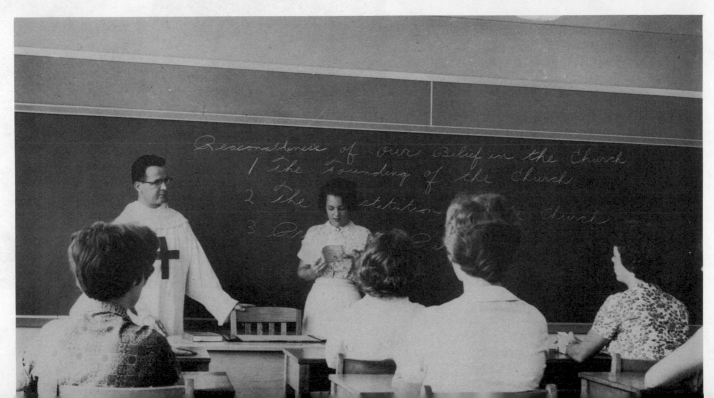

  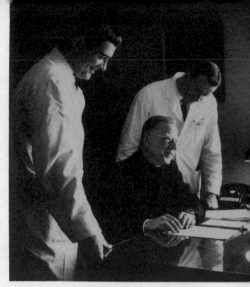

In the field of education a religious priest may be the President and Rector of a college or university,

or a professor of biology,

or the Dean of a college,

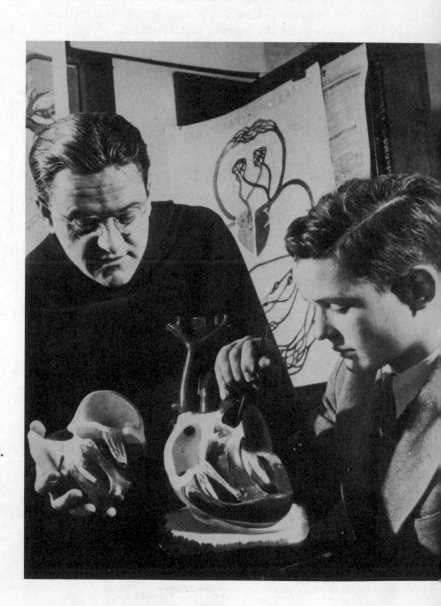

or teach in a Catholic boys' high school.

Sometimes a religious priest may be sent to Rome to do advanced studies,

and there make new friends from all around the world.

These priests may be sometimes assigned to teach in universities, either at home,

or sent abroad to lecture in foreign seminaries.

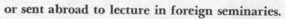

Some priests of religious institutes are assigned to special intellectual apostolates;

some undertake new social works to form the world into a true Christian pattern;

some volunteer to undertake difficult mission assignments to preserve, and enlarge the Church behind the Iron Curtain.

Some priests find themselves drawn towards the work of a chaplain: the chaplain in a prison or penitentiary;

the chaplain in one of the armed services;

the chaplain in a hospital.

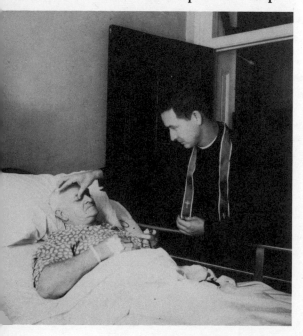

In specialized scientific fields, such as astronomy, priests devote their talents both abroad—

—and in observatories in the United States.

In the arts of communication, especially radio and television, many religious priests have found an outlet for their scientific and artistic talents.

The Priest on the Missions

WHAT is a missionary? He is "one who has been sent." And for what is he sent? In Christianity, the missionary is one sent to proclaim the life and Word of Jesus Christ. In this sense, too, Christ was a missionary from the Father to men. His purpose was to reveal to men the message and gift of Eternal Life.

And Christ gave His mission to His Apostles: "As the Father has sent me, I also send you."

When a missionary departs, as this young man in white kneeling on the right, he goes forth with the blessing of the Church, his superiors, his family and his friends.

The missionary concept of the Catholic Church covers the whole world.

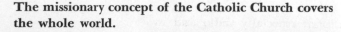

The Catholic missionary goes forth to bring Christ to all men.

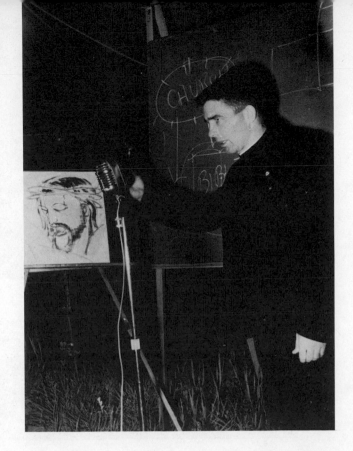

During their summer vacation, seminarians are often called to assist in teaching catechism to children of the same areas.

Catholic religious missionaries preach the Gospel at Tent Meetings in the mountains of the non-Catholic areas of the South.

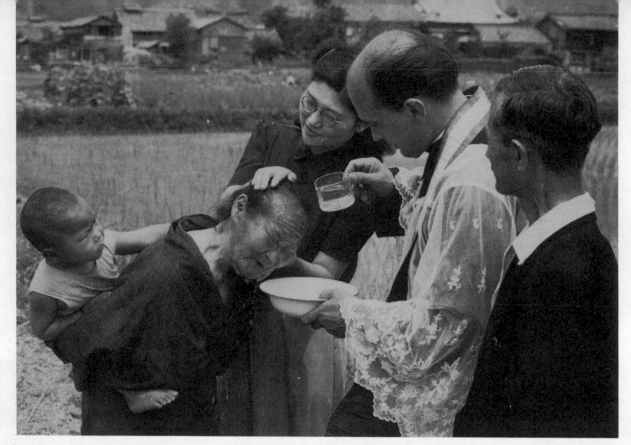

"Go, teach all nations, baptizing them in the name of the Father, and of the Son, and of the Holy Spirit."

"My Flesh is food indeed, given for the life of the world."

To win souls to Christ, the missionary must first show Christ in himself to these souls.

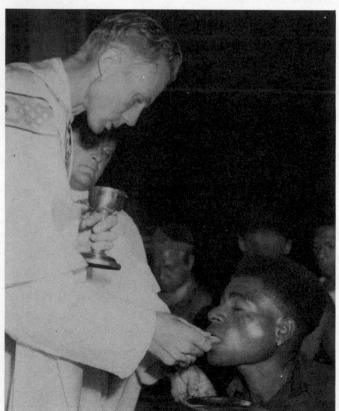

Christ grows in the souls of men through His missionaries; and through the same missionaries, the visible Church springs up everywhere.

The missionary is not a foreigner to his people, he is their Father, because he has shown them Christ and Christ's Church.

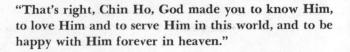

"That's right, Chin Ho, God made you to know Him, to love Him and to serve Him in this world, and to be happy with Him forever in heaven."

All the continents experience the educational influence of the Catholic missionary: Africa,

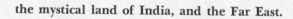

Central and South America.

the mystical land of India, and the Far East.

Through the missionary Christ's blessing comes on every single thing in his peoples' lives; their crops, their children, and their souls.

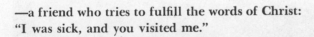

And in sickness and estrangement, such as lepers know, a warm friend is found in their missionary,

—a friend who tries to fulfill the words of Christ: "I was sick, and you visited me."

In the coy eyes of this young Burmese child shines forth the yearning of the nations for Christ: "Won't somebody please introduce us?"

The baby flung on its mother's back is asleep; so are many of the nations of the world in relation to Christ. When there are enough missionaries to send forth, they shall be awakened, even as the child's mother has been. That is why missionaries are sent for, to awaken them to Eternal Life!

And the greatest concern of any missionary priest is always to work for the increase and the development of the native clergy.

The missionary spirit seen in these pages exists in the souls of all priests everywhere. Strange lands and strange people do not make the missionary field, though the foreign field is of great concern.

All priests are sent to Christianize the culture and thinking of the world in which they live.

They are sent out to share with all men the great truths of Jesus Christ, truths that give meaning to every human enterprise. All priests are sent to bring Jesus Christ into their age and city and parish and street through Christ's sacrifice and sacraments, by their words and by their actions.

The Contemplative Vocation

THE contemplative life is a "life hidden with Christ in God." It is a special vocation "to abjection, humility, voluntary poverty, to obedience, peace, joy in the Holy Spirit . . . (It is) the practice of silence, fasting, vigils, prayer, manual labor and above all to follow the more excellent way which is charity." (St. Bernard of Clairvaux).

It is a life of great simplicity composed of three principal divisions which embrace the entire monastic day. First in importance is the 'Opus Dei' or Divine Office, the official prayer of the Church. 'Lectio Divina,' or spiritual reading, informed by prayer, forms the second basic part of the monk's day. And finally manual labor completes the division and includes anything from labor in the fields to the inevitable and necessary tasks of everyday life around the monastery.

In the simplicity and humility of his life the monk discovers the presence of God.

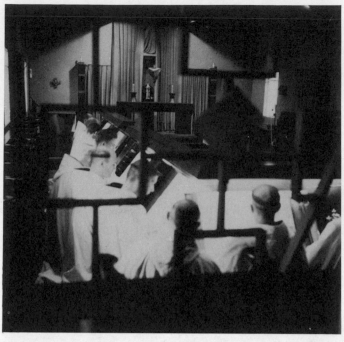

In the early hours of the morning, or after laboring in the heat of the day, the monk leaves his cell to chant the Divine Office.

Throughout the varied course of the day and night, the monastic family unites in choir at various hours to perform the Work of God.

Apart from the Office and manual labor, several hours are set aside each day for Sacred Reading . . .

. . . and for study.

As he reads, writes, or studies, he maintains himself in prolonged contact with God, carrying on his "conversation in Heaven."

The Mass, the same Sacrifice as that of the Cross, assumes a central role in the monk's life, for it is his vocation to live the mystery of the Cross.

The body must also have its food. Even as they partake of this nourishment, the soul also is fed as one of the monks reads aloud from a spiritual book.

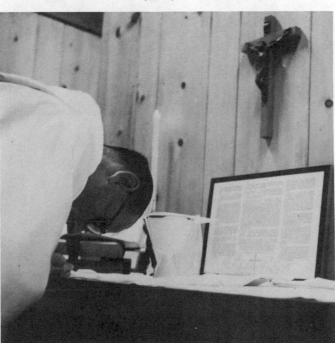

By labor, hard manual labor, the monk supports himself. Each monastery aims at self-support.

They live by the labor of their hands, in the shop . . .

. . . clearing rocks from a field for plowing . . .

. . . tending the bees . . .

. . . jarring the honey . . .

. . . filling the silo.

All this labor is in silence; even the necessary directions are given by signs.

In all these tasks the monk finds God, uniting himself to Him in the secret depths of his heart.

Living in the silence of the cloister, the monk moves always in an atmosphere of prayer. This is his life, minding the things that are above, "hidden with Christ in God."

Epilogue

The Catholic Priest

"I HAVE made myself everybody's servant, to win more souls. I became all things to all men, that I might save all. I do all things for the sake of the gospel. . . . And I will be glad to spend all I have and all I am for your sake." (St. Paul to the Corinthians.)

Almighty God chose every priest from among men that he might be their representative. God issued to each priest He called a very personal invitation, which involves that the priest bind himself forever and without reserve to the service of both God and man.

"The priest is not a priest for himself," the Curé of Ars wrote. "He does not give himself absolution. He does not administer the sacraments to himself. He is not for himself. He is for you."

That there be a strong bond of union between priest and people, St. Paul vigorously exhorted all priests of God to be all things to all men. The priest must identify himself with the people . . . with the needy, with the rejected, with the sinner, and with all who suffer.

God does not set His priest apart by himself. Rather God chooses the priest to exist, to work, and to love God side by side with his people, and as their shepherd to lead them to Himself.

The priest belongs to his people, and to bring them to God he leans completely on the grace and love which is God.

The priest is for others; the priest is for everyone in the world.

Directory

To obtain the information you desire, write to the Director of Vocations at the proper address below:

DIOCESAN CLERGY
See your pastor for details

AFRICAN MISSION FATHERS (S.M.A.)
Queen of Apostles Seminary
Dedham, Mass.

African Missions
23 Bliss Ave.
Tenafly, N. J.

ASSUMPTIONISTS (A.A.)
Assumption College
Worcester 6, Mass.

231 West 14th St.
New York 11, N. Y.

Spalding Lane
Saugerties, N. Y.

**ATONEMENT FRIARS
(GRAYMOOR FRIARS) (S.A.)**
Graymoor Friars
Graymoor
Garrison, N. Y.

AUGUSTINIANS (O.S.A.)
Mother of Good Council Province (West)
St. Monica Seminary
Box 351
Oconomowoc, Wis.

St. Thomas of Villanova Province (East)
Augustinian Fathers
St. Rita's Hall
Villanova, Pa.

BASILIAN FATHERS (C.S.B.)
Basilian Fathers
402 Augustine St.
Rochester 13, N. Y.

St. Michael's College
Toronto, Ontario
Canada

**BASILIAN FATHERS (BYZANTINE RITE)
(O.S.B.M.)**
Basilian Fathers
Mundare, Alberta,
Canada

Basilian Fathers
22 East 7th Street
New York 3, N. Y.

BENEDICTINE FATHERS (O.S.B.)
St. Vincent's Archabbey
Latrobe, Pa.

St. John's Abbey
Collegeville, Minn.

St. Benedict's Abbey
Atchison, Kansas

St. Leo's Abbey
St. Leo, Fla.

Belmont Abbey
Belmont, N. C.

St. Bernard's Abbey
St. Bernard, Ala.

St. Procopius Abbey
Lisle, Ill.

St. Gregory's Abbey
Shawnee, Okla.

Assumption Abbey
Richardton, N. Dak.

St. Bede Abbey
Peru, Ill.

St. Martin's Abbey
Olympia, Washington

Holy Cross Abbey
Canyon City, Colo.

St. Anselm's Abbey
Manchester, N. H.

St. Andrew's Abbey
2900 East Blvd.
Cleveland 4, Ohio

St. Meinrad's Abbey
St. Meinrad, Ind.

Conception Abbey
Conception, Mo.

New Subiaco Abbey
Subiaco, Ark.

St. Joseph's Abbey
St. Benedict, La.

Mt. Angel Abbey
St. Benedict, Ore.

Marmion Abbey
Buterfield Rd.
Aurora, Ill.

St. Benedict's Abbey
Benet Lake, Wis.

St. Pius Monastery
Labadie, Mo.

Blue Cloud Abbey
Marvin, S. Dak.

St. Anselm's Priory
Washington, D. C.

St. Gregory's Priory
Portsmouth, R. I.

St. Louis Priory
Crevecoeur, Mo.

St. Mary's Abbey
528 High Street
Newark 2, N. J.

St. Paul's Abbey
Newton, N. J.

Benedictine Mission Home
Schuyler, Neb.

Mt. Savior Abbey
P. O. Box 272
Elmira, N. Y.

Corpus Christi Priory
Corpus Christi, Texas

BLESSED SACRAMENT FATHERS (S.S.S.)
Blessed Sacrament Fathers
Barre, Mass.

184 East 76th St.
New York 21, N. Y.

Eymard Preparatory Seminary
Hyde Park, N. Y.

**CAMILLIAN FATHERS
(O.S. Cam.)**
5601 Erie St.
Racine, Wisc.

CAPUCHIN-FRANCISCAN, (O.F.M. Cap.)
Province of St. Joseph
Rev. Director of Vocations, O.F.M.Cap.
Capuchin Fathers
1927 North Fourth Street
Milwaukee 12, Wis.
Province of St. Augustine
Rev. Director of Vocations, O.F.M.Cap.
Capuchin Fathers
224 Thirty-Seventh Street
Pittsburgh 1, Pa.
Province of St. Mary
Rev. Director of Vocations, O.F.M.Cap.
Capuchin Fathers
110 Shonnard Place
Yonkers 3, New York
Irish Capuchins
Rev. Director of Vocations, O.F.M.Cap.
St. Francis High School
200 Michigan Avenue
La Canada, California
Italian Capuchins
Custody of the Italian Capuchin Fathers
Rev. Director of Vocations, O.F.M.Cap.
Immaculate Heart of Mary Friary
Lockland Road
Geneva, N. Y.
Polish Capuchins
Province of SS. Adalbert and Stanislaus
Rev. Vocational Director
P. O. Box 142
Broken Arrow, Oklahoma

CARMELITES (O. Carm.)
Province of the Most Pure Heart of Mary
(For the East)
Carmelite Junior Seminary
Hamilton, Mass.
(For the West)
St. Cyril's Monastery
6428 S. Dante Ave.
Chicago 37, Ill.

Mt. Carmel Seminary
Niagara Falls, Ontario,
Canada
Province of St. Elias
(For East)
339 East 28th Street
New York, N. Y.

(For West)
942 W. 70th St.
Los Angeles, Cal.

**CLARETIAN MISSIONARY FATHERS
(C.M.F.)**
St. Jude Seminary
Momence, Ill.

18127 S. Alameda St.
Compton, Cal.

COLUMBAN FATHERS (S.S.C.)
St. Columbans
Milton, Mass.

St. Columbans
Bristol, R. I.

St. Columbans
Silver Creek, N. Y.

St. Columbans
Nebraska

1017 Elden Ave.
Los Angeles, Cal.

2444 Congress St.
N. San Diego, Cal.

869 President St.
Brooklyn, N. Y.

5714 N. Sheridan Rd.
Chicago, Ill.

1344 Summit Ave.
St. Paul, Minn.

115 Presidio Ave.
San Francisco, Cal.

CONSOLATA FATHERS (I.M.C.)
Consolata Mission Seminary
5406 Colorado Ave., N. W.
Washington, D. C.

CROSIER FATHERS (O.S.C.)
Sacred Heart Seminary
Box 265
Auburn Rd.
Fort Wayne, Ind.

DISCALCED CARMELITES (O.C.D.)
(Southern Province)
1125 South Walker St.
Oklahoma City, Oklahoma
(Northern Province)
Discalced Carmelite Monastery
514 Warren St.
Brookline 46, Mass.

DIVINE WORD MISSIONARIES (S.V.D.)
(Western Province)
St. Mary's Mission House
Techny, Ill.
Divine Word Seminary
Perrysburg, Ohio
(Southern Province)
St. Augustine Seminary
Bay St. Louis, Miss.
(Eastern Province)
Sacred Heart Mission House
Girard, Pa.

St. Michael's Juniorate
Conesus, N. Y.

St. Francis Xavier Seminary
Island Creek, Mass.

St. Joseph Mission Seminary
Bordentown, N. J.

Mont St. Jean Baptiste Seminaire
Granby, Quebec,
Canada

**DOMINICAN FATHERS
(O.P.)**
(Province of St. Albert the Great)
Harlem Ave. and Division St.
River Forest, Illinois
(Province of St. Joseph)
869 Lexington Ave.
New York 21, N. Y.
(Province of the Holy Name of Jesus)
2390 Buch St.
San Francisco, Cal.

EDMUNDITES (S.S.E.)
St. Michael's College
Winooski Park, Vermont

St. Edmunds Novitiate
Enders Island
Mystic, Conn.

EUDIST FATHERS (C.J.M.)
Willowbrook Seminary
Hyattsville, Md.
FATHERS OF MERCY (S.P.M.)
11 DeSales Place
Brooklyn 17, N. Y.
Province of SS. Francis and James (Mexico)
Our Lady of Guadalupe Friary
Box 85
Hebbronville, Tex.
FRANCISCANS OF THE SLAV-
BYZANTINE RITE (O.F.M.)
Monastery of Our Lady of Perpetual Help
4 Ponus St.
New Canaan, Conn.
GLENMARY MISSIONERS
Glenmary Missioners
Glendale, Ohio
HOLY CROSS FATHERS (C.S.C.)
(Eastern U. S.)
Seminary of Our Lady of Holy Cross
North Eaton, Mass.
Holy Cross Novitiate
Bennington, Vermont
Holy Cross Fathers
63 North River St.
Wilkes-Barre, Pa.
Holy Cross Fathers
2788 So. Park Ave.
Lackawanna 18, N. Y.
(Western U. S.)
Holy Cross Seminary
Notre Dame, Ind.
Sacred Heart Novitiate
Jordan, Minn.
Holy Cross Fathers
Portland University
Portland 3, Ore.
Holy Cross Fathers
7655 Dempster St.
Niles, Ill.
Foreign Missions of Holy Cross
4301 Harewood Rd., N. E.
Washington 17, D. C.
HOLY FAMILY FATHERS (M.S.F.)
Holy Family Seminary
2500 Ashby Road
St. Louis 14, Mo.
HOLY GHOST FATHERS (C.S.Sp.)
1615 Manchester Lane, N. W.
Washington 11, D. C.
IMMACULATE HEART MISSIONERS
(C.I.C.M.)
Immaculate Heart Mission House
4651 North 25th St.
Arlington 7, Va.
JESUITS (S.J.)
New York Province
501 East Fordham Road
New York 58, N. Y.
Missouri Province
4511 West Pine Blvd.
St. Louis 8, Mo.
New Orleans Province
4133 Banks St.
New Orleans 19, La.
California Province
2460 Lyon St.
San Francisco 23, Calif.
New England Province
297 Commonwealth Ave.
Boston 15, Mass.
Chicago Province
509 North Oak Park Ave.
Oak Park, Ill.
Oregon Province
Oregon Province
615 N. W. 20th Ave.
Portland 9, Ore.
Detroit Province
892 W. Boston Blvd.
Detroit 2, Mich.
Wisconsin Province
3109 N. Lake Drive
Milwaukee 11, Wisc.
Buffalo Province
1180 Delaware Ave.
Buffalo 9, N. Y.
Maryland Province
5704 Roland Ave.
Baltimore 10, Md.
JOSEPHITE FATHERS (S.S.J.)
1130 North Calvert St.
Baltimore 2, Md.

Epiphany Apostolic College
Newburgh, N. Y.
LA SALLETTE MISSIONARIES (M.S.)
85 New Park Ave.
Hartford 6, Conn.
La Salette Seminary
Box 306
Jefferson City, Mo.
FATHERS OF ST. JOSEPH OF MURIALDO
(C.S.J.)
Fathers of St. Joseph of Murialdo
San Jose Parish
Albuquerque, New Mex.
FATHERS OF THE CATHOLIC PRESS
(S.S.P.)
(Pious Society of St. Paul)
2187 Victory Blvd.
Staten Island 2, N. Y.
Queen of Apostles Seminary
Lake Shore Road
Derby, New York
St. Paul's Monastery
Canfield, Ohio
FATHERS OF THE SACRED HEARTS
(SS.CC.)
Sacred Heart Monastery
17 Adams St.
Fairhaven, Mass.
FRANCISCAN FATHERS (O.F.M.Conv.)
Vocation Director
812 North Salina St.
Syracuse 8, New York
Vocational Director
566 Front St.
Chicopee, Mass.
Vocation Director
955 Ringwood Rd.
Lake Forest, Ill.
Vocation Director
Mt. St. Francis Seminary
Mt. St. Francis, Indiana
FRANCISCAN FATHERS (T.O.R.)
Province of the Most Sacred Heart of Jesus
Director of Vocations
Mount Assisi Monastery
Loretto, Penn.
Province of the Immaculate Conception
St. Bernardine's Monastery
Hollidaysburg, Pa.
Commissariat (Spanish Fathers)
St. Joseph's Convent
212 Lafayette St.
Newark, N. J.
Commissariat (Croatian Fathers)
St. Nicholas Convent
24 Maryland Ave.
Millvale, Pa.
FRANCISCAN FATHERS (O.F.M.)
Province of the Most Holy Name of Jesus
St. Joseph's Seraphic Seminary
Callicoon, N. Y.
Province of St. John the Baptist
1615 Vine St.
Cincinnati 10, Ohio
Province of the Sacred Heart of Jesus
St. Joseph's Seminary
Westmont, Ill.
Province of Santa Barbara
St. Boniface Friary
133 Golden Gate Avenue
San Francisco 2, Cal.
Province of the Assumption of B. V. M.
Franciscan Fathers
Pulaski, Wisconsin
Province of the Immaculate Conception
10 S. 10th Ave.
Mount Vernon, N. Y.
Commissariat of the Holy Land (For Work
in the Holy Land and in the Near East)
Mt. St. Sepulchre
1400 Quincey St., N. E.
Washington 17, D. C.
Commissariat of the Holy Cross
P. O. Box 608
Lemont, Ill.
Commissariat of the Most Holy Saviour
Holy Family Monastery
232 S. Home Ave.
Pittsburgh, Pa.
Commissariat of St. John Capistran
Assumption Friary
Knickerbocker Road
Roebling, N. J.
Commissariat of St. Stephen
838 King's Highway
Bridgeport, Conn.

Commissariat of the Holy Family
4851 Drexel Blvd.
Chicago, Ill.
Commissariat of St. Casimir
Franciscan Fathers
Kennebunkport, Me.
U. S. Foundations of Mexican Provinces
Province of the Holy Gospel (Mexico)
Roger Bacon College
2400 Marr St.
El Paso, Tex.
Province of SS. Peter and Paul (Mexico)
St. Anthony Seminary
Las Cruces, N. M.
MARIAN FATHERS (M.I.C.)
2327 W. 23rd Place
Chicago 8, Ill.
Marian Fathers Novitiate
Clarendon Hill, Ill.
Marian Fathers
Eden Hill
Stockbridge, Mass.
MARIANISTS (S.M.)
Cincinnati Province
Mount St. John
4370 Patterson Rd.
Dayton 10, Ohio
St. Louis Province
Maryhurst Normal
1101 S. Lindbergh Blvd.
Kirkwood 22, Mo.
Pacific Province
The Marianists
P. O. 586
Santa Cruz, Cal.
MARIANNHILL FATHERS (C.M.M.)
St. Bernard's Seminary
23601 Ann Arbor Trail
Dearborn, Michigan
MARIST FATHERS (S.M.)
Harewood Road, N. E.
Washington 17, D. C.
St. Mary's Manor
Penndel, Pa.
27 Isabella St.
Boston 16, Mass.
St. Peter Chanel Seminary
1675 Grand Ave.
San Rafael, Calif.
MARYKNOLL FATHERS (M.M.)
Maryknoll P. O.
Maryknoll, N. Y.
MILL HILL FATHERS (M.H.F.)
R. D. 1
Slingerlands, N. Y.
MISSIONARIES OF ST. CHARLES
(P.S.S.C.)
208 Flagg Place
Staten Island 4, N. Y.
Sacred Heart Seminary
Melrose Park, Ill.
MISSIONARIES OF SS. PETER AND PAUL
(P.I.M.E.)
121 E. Boston Blvd.
Detroit 2, Mich.
MISSIONARY SERVANTS OF THE MOST
HOLY TRINITY (M.S.SS.T.)
P. O. Box 30
Holy Trinity Heights
Silver Spring, Md.
MONTFORT FATHERS (S.M.M.)
Montfort Preparatory Seminary
Bay Shore, N. Y.
NORBERTINES (O. Praem.)
St. Norbert Abbey
West De Pere, Wis.
Our Lady of Daylesford Priory
Box 566
Paoli, Pa.
OBLATE FATHERS (O.M.I.)
First American Province
225 Fargo Ave.
Buffalo 13, N. Y.
Our Lady of Hope Seminary
Box 708
Newburgh, N. Y.
Second American Province
1900 McCullough Ave.
San Antonio, Tex.
St. John Baptist Province (French-speaking)
725 Merrimack St.
Lowell, Mass.
St. Henry Province
5901 West Main St.
Belleville, Ill.

127

OBLATES OF ST. FRANCIS DE SALES
(O.S.F.S.)
2200 Kentnere Parkway
Wilmington 6, Delaware
Oblate Novitiate
Childs, Md.
OBLATE OF ST. JOSEPH (O.S.J.)
Oblates of St. Joseph
808 Susquehanna Ave.
West Pittston, Pa.
Oblates of St. Joseph
544 West Cliff Drive
Santa Cruz, Calif.
St. Joseph's House of Studies
1323 Quincy St., N. E.
Washington 17, D. C.
St. Joseph's Summer College
Fishers Landing, N. Y.
ORATORIAN FATHERS (C.O.)
Box 895
Rock Hill, S. C.
ORDER OF OUR LADY OF MERCY
(O.D.M.)
Monastery of Our Lady of Mercy
R. F. D. 2
Middleburg Heights, Ohio
PALLOTTINE FATHERS (S.A.C.)
5424 Bluemound Road
Milwaukee 13, Wis.
309 North Paca Street
Baltimore, 1, Maryland
PASSIONIST FATHERS (C.P.)
(For the East)
Holy Cross Preparatory Seminary
Dunkirk, N. Y.
(For the West)
Passionist Preparatory Seminary
Warrentown, Mo.
PAULIST FATHERS (C.S.P.)
St. Paul's College
Washington 17, D. C.
415 West 59th St.
New York 19, N. Y.
PIARIST FATHERS (S.P.)
P. O. Box 2096
Buffalo 5, N. Y.
PRECIOUS BLOOD FATHERS (C.PP.S.)
Priesthood Students:
Brunnerdale Seminary
Canton, Ohio
REDEMPTIONIST FATHERS (C.SS.R.)
5 East 74th St.
New York 21, N. Y.
1118 N. Grand Blvd.
St. Louis 6, Mo.
Villa San Clemente
Livermore, Calif.
RESURRECTION FATHERS (C.R.)
2249 North Lockwood Ave.
Chicago 39, Ill.
SACRED HEART FATHERS (S.C.J.)
Divine Heart Seminary
Donaldson, Ind.

Dehon Seminary of the Sacred Heart
Great Barrington, Mass.
Sacred Heart Mission House
Sainte Marie, Ill.
SACRED HEART MISSIONARIES
(M.S.C.)
719 Batavia Ave.
Geneva, Ill.
3014 Logan Ave.
Youngstown 4, Ohio
Sacred Heart Seminary
Shelby, Ohio
SALESIANS OF ST. JOHN BOSCO (S.D.B.)
Eastern Province
(For Priesthood)
148 Main St.
New Rochelle, N. Y.
P. O. Box 545
West Haverstraw, N. Y.
(Veterans and late vocations)
Don Bosco College
Newton, N. J.
Western Province
2851 North Ave.
Richmond, Calif.
(Veterans and late vocations)
Salesian College
Aptos, Cal.
SALVATORIAN FATHERS (S.D.S.)
Salvatorian Seminary
St. Nazianz, Wisconsin
Mother of the Savior Seminary
Blackwood, New Jersey
Jordan Seminary
Menominee, Michigan
St. Pius X Seminary
Rio Dell, California
Trinity College
Sioux City, Iowa
SERVITE FATHERS (O.S.M.)
3121 Jackson Blvd.
Chicago 12, Ill.
SONS OF MARY, HEALTH OF THE SICK
(F.M.S.I.)
Sylva Maria
Salem End Road
Framingham, Mass.
STIGMATINE FATHERS (C.P.S.)
900 Washington St.
Wellesley 81, Mass.
SULPICIANS (S.S.)
St. Mary's Seminary
Baltimore 10, Md.
SYLVESTRINE-BENEDICTINES (O.S.B.)
17320 Rosemont Road
Detroit 19, Mich.
THEATINE FATHERS (C.R.)
1050 S. Birch St.
Denver 22, Colo.
TRAPPISTS (O.C.S.O.)
Our Lady of Gethsemani Abbey
Trappist, Kentucky

Our Lady of New Melleray Abbey
Dubuque, Iowa
Saint Joseph's Abbey
Spencer, Massachusetts
Our Lady of the Holy Ghost Abbey
Route 1
Conyers, Georgia
Our Lady of the Holy Trinity Abbey
P. O. Box 105
Huntsville, Utah
Our Lady of Guadalupe Abbey
P. O. Box 207
Lafayette, Oregon
Our Lady of Mepkin Abbey
Moncks Corner
South Carolina
Our Lady of the Holy Cross Monastery
Berryville, Virginia
Our Lady of the Genesee Abbey
Piffard, New York
Our Lady of the Assumption Monastery
Sweden, Missouri
Our Lady of New Clairvaux Monastery
Vina, California
Our Lady of Colorado Monastery
Aspen, Colorado
TRINITARIANS (O.SS.T)
Sacred-Heart Monastery
Pikesville 8, Md.
4301 Madison St.
Hyattsville, Md.
VERONA FATHERS (F.S.C.J.)
8108 Beechmont Ave.
Cincinnati 3, Ohio
VINCENTIANS (C.M.)
500 E. Chelten Ave.
Philadelphia 44, Pa.
St. Vincent's Seminary
127th St. & Archer Ave.
Lemont, Ill.
WHITE FATHERS (W.F.)
6027 N. Sheridan Road
Chicago, Ill.
328 S. Virgil Ave.
Los Angeles, Cal.
1624 - 21st St., N. W.
Washington 9, D. C.
Our Lady of River Ridge Seminary
Franklin, Pa.
White Fathers Novitiate
Alexandria Bay, N. Y.
XAVERIAN MISSIONARY FATHERS
(S.X.)
101 Summer St.
Holliston, Mass.
SCHOOL OF ST. PHILIP NERI (FOR
DELAYED VOCATIONS)
126 Newbury Street
Boston, Mass.

Index of Religious Institutes According to Proper Initials